AFTER THE END

Dennis Kelly

AFTER THE END

OBERON BOOKS
LONDON

WWW.OBERONBOOKS.COM

First published in 2005 by Oberon Books Ltd
521 Caledonian Road, London N7 9RH
Tel: +44 (0) 20 7607 3637 / Fax: +44 (0) 20 7607 3629
e-mail: info@oberonbooks.com
www.oberonbooks.com

A catalogue record for this book is available from the British
Library.

PB ISBN: 9781840025804
E ISBN: 9781849431743

Cover image: Getty Images / Cog Design

Printed and bound by CPI Group (UK) Ltd, Croydon, CR0 4YY.

Visit www.oberonbooks.com to read more about all our books
and to buy them. You will also find features, author interviews and
news of any author events, and you can sign up for e-newsletters
so that you're always first to hear about our new releases.

Characters

MARK

LOUISE

After the End was first produced at The Bush Theatre, in a Paines Plough / Bush Theatre co-production, on 28 July 2005, with the following cast:

MARK, Tom Brooke

LOUISE, Kerry Condon

Director Roxana Silbert
Designer Miriam Buether
Lighting Design Chahine Yavroyan
Sound Design Matt McKenzie

Beginning

MARK and LOUISE. A 1980s nuclear fallout shelter with a wheel-hatch in the ceiling, but in the present day. Bunks, table and chair, toilet area off and large metallic chest under the beds.

Pause.

MARK: I'm carrying you. I can't find my way because the streets, the houses, the houses were gone, the buildings were rubble, so I couldn't be sure and I'm panicking, I'm scared, there's bodies everywhere and just, the only sound is things burning and I can see the cloud rising and there was fires inside the, the cloud, inside it, beautiful, just unbelievable just, and I got to the junction and I thought 'Is this the fucking Junction?' there was no land marks, this is my fucking road and I've lived here for years but I didn't know if this was my fucking road even though I've lived here for years and I put you down next to this burnt lump, this body, charred, completely, like burnt wood, you know when it gets charred and it's cracked and you can break off a piece of charcoal, no skin, no clothes and her hands were almost ash, there was bits of her blowing away and I put you down next to this. And I'm clambering over the rubble trying to get higher to see if this is the fucking junction because if this isn't the fucking junction we're fucked, we're really fucked, the cloud is the only thing I can see above the fire and smoke and rubble and it's like it's rising with me and I'm thinking, okay, we've survived the blast, miracle, we've survived the fireball, miracle, but when that cloud starts to fall we're fucked, we're fucked, we're fucked unless we're in here. And then I see next door's…pattern on his drive, on his patio, it's a pattern, irregular sort of, it's a pattern but in the bit you walk on –

LOUISE: Crazy paving.

MARK: Yes, his crazy, yes, paving, his, yes, and I go back to you and I get there and the body is lifting itself up.

It's pushing itself up. It's trying to push itself, but it's crumbling. It's pushing itself up and its fingers are crumbling and it's pushing itself up on its palms but its palms are crumbling, but it's still pushing itself and a bit by the elbow breaks off and I can see meat and bone and I run. I run off. I ran off and left you there.

LOUISE: But you came back.

MARK: Yes. I saw the crazy paving and I came back. And I picked you up. And I brought you here.

Beat.

LOUISE: Thank you.

MARK: You're welcome.

Silence.

LOUISE: But I'm starting my new job on Monday.

MARK: Yeah, well that's –

I think that's probably…

Yeah, no.

* * *

MARK is pulling cans and supplies out of the metal chest, talking to LOUISE over his shoulder. She sits staring at him, lost in thought.

MARK: Chilli…

Chilli…

Chilli…

Baked beans, baked beans with sausages…

Chilli…

Tuna…

More tuna, with mayonnaise, I don't think that's very –

Chilli…

She gets up and comes over to him.

LOUISE: I've got your number.

Beat.

MARK: What?

LOUISE: I wasn't leaving without, I mean I've got your number, Mark.

MARK: Oh, I know.

LOUISE: I've got your

MARK: Oh, I know, I know

LOUISE: coz I feel I didn't really, last night I didn't really

MARK: Leaving does are always

LOUISE: I didn't really, they are, yeah, leaving does are always, did I talk to you? because

MARK: we talked

LOUISE: We did, yeah, that's right, but, because I don't think I got the chance to talk to you properly last night

MARK: Oh, no, no, you had lots, I mean you had lots, loads of people, you can't

LOUISE: I wasn't just gonna, but I'm saying I had your number, so it's not as if

MARK: Oh God no.

LOUISE: I mean I wasn't, I don't really remember

MARK: no, no, I know, well, you were a bit

LOUISE: I was but, I wasn't just never ever again or something, I mean

MARK: No, we're friends, Jesus, no, I know

LOUISE: Just so you know.

MARK: Oh I do know, definitely.

LOUISE: Do you?

MARK: Definitely. We're friends, I mean, we're friends it's not just

LOUISE: Exactly. Definitely.

Beat.

Did we row a little?

MARK: No.

LOUISE: Did we?

MARK: No, no, well…

LOUISE: We did, didn't we. God, not again.

MARK: Well, yes, we did a little.

LOUISE: (*Laughing a little.*) Jesus, sorry

MARK: (*Laughing with her.*) no, no, it was just

LOUISE: We're like kids or something, God, I'm sorry, was I an arsehole?

MARK: no, honestly it was about nothing

LOUISE: my memory is like in and out, was it about nothing? what was it about?

MARK: Nothing.

LOUISE: Really?

MARK: it was about nothing, I mean so small, nothing at all

LOUISE: Jesus, just arguing over nothing

MARK: honestly don't worry

LOUISE: like kids or something,

MARK: and you'd had a few

LOUISE: someone should smack us across the back of the legs

MARK: so I know you didn't mean anything

LOUISE: I really didn't, God I'm sorry

MARK: because, no, don't apologise because I'm saying, I know you didn't mean

LOUISE: I didn't.

MARK: to be rude

LOUISE: I wasn't rude.

MARK: You called me a cunt.

Beat.

LOUISE: That was rude.

MARK: It was a little.

LOUISE: Sorry.

MARK: It was a little

LOUISE: Yeah, I know, I'm sorry, I really am, fucking hell, I really am

MARK: Oh look, I don't think you meant it to be so

LOUISE: when I have a few

MARK: cruel

LOUISE: Cruel?

MARK: or harsh, I mean

LOUISE: it was more like you're a cunt or something, like you just call someone a cunt and you don't really mean

MARK: You remember?

LOUISE: Pieces, I remember

MARK: that's why I left the pub after you, to say

LOUISE: I don't remember leaving, Jesus,

MARK: I wanted to say sorry, or, and that's when

LOUISE: it happened?

MARK: when it happened, yes, so we were lucky, when you think about it, we were lucky we rowed

LOUISE: Rowing as a good thing?

MARK: rowing as a good thing, yeah, exactly, because I think we were sheltered by, wall, a wall or something so –

Look, let's leave it, we need to get on. Imperative, so

LOUISE: Exactly.

Jesus Christ, yeah, exactly.

Pause.

But I'm just saying that I wasn't fucking off and not saying goodbye, because I have your number so I wasn't actually saying goodbye.

MARK: I never feel like I'm saying goodbye to someone I really like.

LOUISE: Exactly. That's exactly, that's how I feel.

MARK: I'm really glad we talked about this.

He goes back to sorting.

LOUISE: D'you want a hand?

MARK: What?

LOUISE: Sorting or…

MARK: No it's fine I've…

LOUISE: I could help

MARK: got it all

LOUISE: I could help or something.

Beat.

MARK: Yeah. Yeah, okay. I'm, well I'm just sorting it into

LOUISE: Rations?

MARK: rations, yeah, it's rations, yeah, that's right, it's rations really.

LOUISE: So it's days of the week?

MARK: Yeah, and different foodstuffs, varied, variations. We're a bit short on food. We'll be fine. I mean there's enough for one comfortably and we can stretch, we can make it –

LOUISE: My brother's dead.

D'you think my brother's –

Probably.

Don't feel

anything.

Pause.

MARK: D'you think you're suppressing…

LOUISE: No. I just don't feel anything.

MARK: I cried.

LOUISE: Did you?

MARK: Sorry. I don't know why I said that, sorry, shit. Before you came round. Maybe relief at getting in out of, or something.

LOUISE: maybe I'm concussed

MARK: I don't think that affects your feelings.

LOUISE: What was it?

She sits down and starts sorting with him.

Do you know?

MARK: Terrorists. Probably.

It was small. It looked smaller than, I dunno, but I mean it must've, so…

Suitcase nuke.

LOUISE: In a suitcase?

MARK: No, no, they just,

LOUISE: How do you know it was in…?

MARK: No, it wasn't, no, that's what they call them. You know, they're like a portable device that you set off yourself. That's why they say suitcase because like maybe you could carry one in

LOUISE: Right. Why is there nothing on the radio?

MARK: Could be anything.

LOUISE: Like what?

MARK: EMP.

LOUISE: What's that?

MARK: Electro magnetic pulse. Maybe. Knocks out all electrics in a certain area, maybe the masts, the transmitters

LOUISE: Is that likely?

MARK: No.

Beat.

We'll keep trying.

LOUISE: Every three hours. That's what you said.

MARK: Yeah. Every three

LOUISE: I'm glad you know about this stuff, Mark.

MARK: Ah, yeah. Well, you know. My shelter. So…

LOUISE: So is this the menu for the next two weeks?

MARK: Yes. Two weeks.

Sorry. There's a lot of chilli.

LOUISE: I like Chilli. We can heat the shelter at the same time.

MARK: Yeah.

Beat.

How?

LOUISE: With all the farting.

Beat.

It's a joke.

MARK: Oh yeah.

He laughs. She smiles. They carry on sorting. Suddenly he makes a farting noise. It is not funny, but she laughs anyway.

LOUISE: You were right.

I mean all this. Shelter and –

MARK: Louise –

LOUISE: You were though, weren't you. We all took the piss. We laughed when you bought a flat with a shelter in the garden

MARK: Christ, that doesn't matter now, and that isn't, actually – I keep saying this – that isn't why I bought the flat

LOUISE: I know

MARK: I bought the flat because I like it and it's not too bad for transport and it happened to have an old shelter in the back

LOUISE: Yeah, but you kept it.

MARK: I kept it, yes, rather than tear out

LOUISE: You kept it stocked up. In preparation –

MARK: Which I kept stocked up because the world has gone fucking insane!

They sort.

Look, it wasn't about the shelter. It was because I got the shelter. I mean if it'd been someone else everyone'd be all 'Oh, isn't that great, isn't that funny' and all that old whatever, but because I get it

LOUISE: Oh, come on.

MARK: What?

LOUISE: Oh, come on Mark, that's not true.

MARK: It is. I mean I'm not being, it is, because if Francis had got it everyone'd think it was hilarious and really clever but because it's me

LOUISE: Mark, it just seemed a bit

MARK: What?

LOUISE: a bit, well, paranoid.

MARK: Paranoid? They've let off a nuclear bomb!

LOUISE: I know, okay, I'm saying it seemed, at the time it seemed

MARK: Well it seemed wrong, then, didn't it.

LOUISE: That's what I'm saying, I'm saying you were right.

MARK: Right but paranoid.

LOUISE: Because, alright, but some of the things you say sometimes

MARK: are right, were right, have turned out right.

LOUISE: Well, maybe they are

MARK: Well, who do you think did this then?

LOUISE: I know, I'm saying

MARK: Well I tell you what, whoever it was, you can bet your life they had beards.

LOUISE: Oh, Mark.

MARK: Alright, sorry, no I mean, fair enough

LOUISE: For Christ's sake

MARK: Well, actually, now that we're at it, who do you think did this?

LOUISE: I know, Mark, that's what I'm saying, I'm confused, I don't fucking know, but what I'm saying is

MARK: What?

Beat.

LOUISE: Look, there's all these people, right, who are just fucking saying I know what's best and you do what I say or I'll shoot you in the fucking head, on both sides, Mark, on both fucking sides, and I just don't think that the best way to combat them is to start saying you do what I say or I'll shoot you in the fucking head.

MARK: How do you fight, then?

LOUISE: I don't –

MARK: No, I'm interested.

LOUISE: I don't know, Mark, I'm saying I'm confused, I'm saying this is what I believe and meanwhile my friends are either dead or screaming in agony or

MARK: Because that's called burying your head in the sand. I'm sorry, but it is.

LOUISE: Oh, for fuck's sake.

MARK: Which is what I refused to do and which is what I was laughed at for.

LOUISE: You weren't laughed at

MARK: and you can sit there and criticise governments and politicians and whatever, and that's easy, to do from pubs and trendy bars and sitting rooms, but at the end of the day you have to do something, the reality is tough, you have to close borders, imprison if you have to

LOUISE: Jesus, Mark, you're sounding just a little bit fascist.

MARK: And that is exactly, that is exactly the kind of comment and attitude

LOUISE: I don't mean –

MARK: It's a war! It's a war and just because there hadn't been an attack like this didn't mean there wasn't going to be, and what do you want to do with that time, just sit and accept

LOUISE: I know

MARK: just wait there drinking, laughing, smoking, taking the piss

LOUISE: I know, Mark, I'm saying

MARK: Look at where we are!

LOUISE: I'm saying I fucking know, for fuck's sake, I'm saying I fucking –

MARK: Well don't start swearing at me all over again!

They sort in silence.

LOUISE: I'm saying I know.

They sort.

Did you hurt your back?

MARK: What?

LOUISE: Did you hurt your back, Mark?

MARK: Well, I think

LOUISE: What?

MARK: I think I grazed it.

LOUISE: Why didn't you tell me?

MARK: I don't know, I –

LOUISE: Let me see it. Let me see it!

He turns round and lifts his shirt at the back.

Jesus.

MARK: It's nothing it's –

She touches it.

Ow!

LOUISE: Looks like a burn.

She goes to the chest, pulls out some ointment and bandages. She is at his back, starts treating him.

Is it radiation or…?

MARK: Don't remember, I mean it was all, maybe it's a graze

LOUISE: It's a burn.

MARK: getting you in, it's a tight, maybe I grazed –

LOUISE: It's a fucking burn, Mark.

Looks sore.

MARK: It's a little –

Ow.

Yes, it's a little.

LOUISE: You should've told me. You fucking tell me about things like this.

MARK: Okay.

LOUISE: You fucking tell me. I mean it, Mark, you fucking –

MARK: Okay!

Pause.

LOUISE: Okay?

MARK: Okay.

She has finished. He turns around.

You know, I think we're going to be alright.

* * *

They lie on their bunks, wrapped up, cold.

MARK: Cold.

LOUISE: Yeah.

Beat.

MARK: We have to save the gas. I'm not being bossy, Louise.

LOUISE: Oh, I know.

MARK: and the fumes are not so, so it's best

LOUISE: We're fine like this.

MARK: Yeah.

Yeah, fine like this.

Pause.

And sorry about the water as well

LOUISE: Oh, no don't

MARK: I mean I wasn't being

LOUISE: Oh, I know, Mark

MARK: bossy or, we just have to save

LOUISE: I know you weren't, and I didn't mean

MARK: because we can't really use it for

LOUISE: I didn't mean to snap

MARK: washing, you didn't snap.

LOUISE: I did and I'm sorry.

MARK: No, course you didn't.

LOUISE: I mean drinking's more important.

MARK: It is.

> Maybe we could wash a little, though. Special occasions. You didn't snap.
>
> *Silence.*
>
> Are you thinking about Francis?

LOUISE: What?

MARK: No, I mean, you know. Are you?

LOUISE: Am I thinking about Francis?

MARK: Because I just noticed in the pub –

LOUISE: What?

MARK: No, I mean I just noticed that you were friendly.

LOUISE: Well, we're friends

MARK: with him, oh no, I know, I mean…no, no, I'm just saying in case you wanted

LOUISE: What?

MARK: To talk. I thought you might want to talk about it. Or something.

LOUISE: D'you think he's dead?

No answer.

I'm really glad you brought this flat, you know.

MARK: Well. You know what we say in the reprographics department; tedious but lucrative.

Pause.

Are you thinking about Francis? Coz I mean if you wanted to talk –

LOUISE: I'm thinking about my brother.

MARK: Right.

D'you want to talk, or…

LOUISE: No. Thank you.

Silence. He has an idea.

MARK: They send the first two astronauts to Mars, right, and they're in their little – it's a man and a woman – they're in their little unit and it's a six-month flight to get there and they've been crammed into this capsule for six months together, a man and a woman, and they're there in their little unit and it's the first night and the heating's broken down and they're in their bunks freezing away, she's on the top bunk and he's on the bottom bunk and they're both really cold and it's really quiet and they're both not saying anything and after a while she says, 'I'm cold' and he says 'Yeah, me too' and there's a silence and she leans over the bunk and says to him 'Would you get me another blanket?' and he looks up at her and he says 'You know, just for tonight, why don't we pretend like we're man and wife?' And she looks at him and she thinks and she says 'Yeah. Okay. Just for tonight' and he says 'Good. Now get your own damn blanket.'

Pause. He laughs a little to indicate it was a joke. Nothing.

It was a joke, it was…

Pause.

Shit. Sorry.

Fuck, sorry.

I'm sorry, Louise, it's, I wasn't, it's, I wasn't, I wasn't –

LOUISE: Fucking hell, Mark.

MARK: Oh my God I am so

LOUISE: Jesus, where did you get that one?

MARK: Louise, I am so, so…sorry, I am

LOUISE: That's fucking terrible.

She starts laughing.

MARK: I don't know why I said

Laughing harder.

Louise?

LOUISE: That's the most stupid fucking, inappropriate

She can't stop laughing.

MARK: Louise?

LOUISE: You're so mental.

Doesn't know how to take this. Decides it's positive. Starts laughing as well.

MARK: Yeah.

Yeah I know.

They are both laughing.

Fucking mental.

The laughter subsides. Silence.

I touched your breast.

LOUISE: (*Beat.*) What?

MARK: By accident. I didn't mean to it was, I was carrying you and your arm was hanging down and I realised where I was holding you and it was your breast.

I just wanted to say I'm sorry, and for it to be, well, open or

LOUISE: Right.

MARK: It wasn't anything like that, I just couldn't move my arm, because the cloud and, oh fuck, why am I saying this?

LOUISE: Why are you saying this?

MARK: I just wanted –

LOUISE: It's okay.

MARK: shit, I just wanted

LOUISE: Go to sleep, Mark.

MARK: That's a good idea, sleep, yes. Good.

Silence.

LOUISE: What do you think's out there? Now? I mean people and that. I mean d'you think there's people dying up there and –

There is, isn't there.

MARK: Best not to think.

LOUISE: No. No, sorry.

MARK: Enough on our plates.

LOUISE: Yeah. What's it going to be like after? I mean d'you think we'll all be like, will it be the end of things, will it be really military or, I mean will it be like checkpoints and things?

MARK: Dunno.

LOUISE: Will we just have to imprison people if we're suspicious of them or something, I mean will we all be bastards?

MARK: I think we'll take...precautions.

LOUISE: D'you think there's people searching?

MARK: Not yet. Not for a long time yet.

LOUISE: So people are just going to be lying up there? Dying. Screaming.

Beat.

MARK: Best not think about out there. Got to concentrate on getting through. Hard enough in here, eh. We'll be fine, but...best not think about that, out there.

Silence. Another idea.

There are these three vets, right and one's – veterinary surgeons – and one's an – not like veterans, army or, but you probably know that – so one's an alcoholic, one's a drug addict and the other is addicted to pornography and when they get paid the first vet says to the second vet 'Right, I've got this idea' he –

Beat. He looks over. She is crying. He immediately gets off his bunk and sits on the edge of hers. Puts his arm around her. She leans into him.

There, there.

There, there.

Middle

LOUISE: I hate it.

MARK: Well you haven't –

LOUISE: I fucking hate it.

MARK: That's a bit

LOUISE: I fucking

MARK: negative.

LOUISE: hate it.

MARK: Why don't you just –

LOUISE: because I fucking –

MARK: You didn't let me finish my sentence, Louise!

Beat.

LOUISE: Finish your sentence, then.

MARK: Why don't you just try it?

LOUISE: Because I fucking hate it.

Pause.

MARK: We have to do something.

LOUISE: Not that.

MARK: We have to keep occupied, do things.

LOUISE: Not Dungeons and fucking Dragons. Do you play that?

MARK: No, when I was a kid –

LOUISE: Do you dress up like a pixie or something?

MARK: No, no, for God's sake, Louise and I mean you don't dress up you just, look, I'm just, it's just a suggestion because we –

LOUISE: Why haven't you got any other games?

MARK: It was built in the eighties. It's an eighties game.

LOUISE: You brought it two years ago, why aren't there games from other eras, why aren't there some nineties games?

MARK: It seemed sort of – what nineties games?

LOUISE: Pictionary.

MARK: fitting, it sort of fitted with, you know, the, the

LOUISE: Apocalyptic

MARK: nuclear, because, no not, because when I was a kid

LOUISE: You're not a kid.

MARK: I know, but when –

LOUISE: So you shouldn't be playing Dungeons and fucking Dragons.

Beat.

When can we try the radio?

MARK: We tried it two hours ago.

LOUISE: What I said was when can we –

MARK: What's three minus two?

LOUISE: One.

MARK: You can try the radio in one hour then.

LOUISE: I don't have a watch.

MARK: I do, I can tell you.

LOUISE: It's like time's turned off. Doesn't it bother you that there's nothing on the radio?

MARK: I've made you a character, she's an elf called –

LOUISE: I don't want to be a fucking elf!

MARK: You could be a dwarf.

I think you're being negative.

Beat.

Yes. Yes, actually, it bothers me. But what am I going to do about it?

Beat.

LOUISE: Sorry.

MARK: It's only been three days

LOUISE: Feels like three years.

MARK: We have to look after each other.

LOUISE: I know.

I know. I'm sorry, Mark.

Pause.

MARK: When I was a kid I used to love it. Alright, yes, I'm admitting –

Escape or something, I don't…

I associate it with caravans. I've never been in a caravan. I think it was because a mate of mine used to go on holiday in a caravan and we never went on holiday and I always thought what it'd be like to be in a caravan. He'd always tell me stories of getting a girlfriend in this caravan –

LOUISE: This isn't a caravan.

And I'm not your girlfriend.

Silence.

MARK: Would you do it if Francis asked you?

LOUISE: Oh, for God's sake

MARK: No, I'm just wondering

LOUISE: No you're not

MARK: I am

LOUISE: You're not because you're mental and that's a loaded question designed to feed into your paranoia about Francis.

MARK: I don't have paranoia about Francis and this is, actually this is just like Jess' party.

Beat.

LOUISE: Jess' party?

MARK: Yes.

LOUISE: Jess' party?

MARK: Yes.

LOUISE: Why are you bringing up Jess' party?

MARK: Because –

LOUISE: What the fuck has Jess' party got to do with anything?

MARK: Because at Jess' party, at Jess' party you were taking the piss

LOUISE: that was months ago, I mean do you ever let go of anything?

MARK: taking the piss and belittling, you were –

LOUISE: I was belittling?

MARK: Yes, you were belittling me.

LOUISE: At Jess' party, I was belittling you?

MARK: Yes.

LOUISE: What about you!

MARK: What about me?

LOUISE: You were acting like a freak.

MARK: Me?

LOUISE: Like we're all having a drink and a laugh and suddenly everything I say you're like jumping on, no you don't really think that Louise, that's not you Louise, why are you talking about Footballer's Wives, Louise.

MARK: You were being fake.

LOUISE: Fake?

MARK: You were pissed though, so I

LOUISE: Fake? Who the fuck are you to decide if I'm fake or not?

MARK: You weren't being you.

LOUISE: You don't decide who I am, I decide

MARK: We'd talked, when you first started, we'd talked about so many

LOUISE: And I enjoyed those, I mean I really, we had some good

MARK: Stuff that matters, like

LOUISE: And I do, I like that, but who the fuck are you to decide who I am

MARK: cloning and global, and now you're talking about this irrelevant

LOUISE: I was just being normal, getting on with people –

MARK: Upgrading.

LOUISE: (*Beat.*) What?

MARK: You were upgrading.

LOUISE: Oh, for fuck's sake.

MARK: No, its fine, that's what happens, people want more, better friends and

LOUISE: For fuck's sake!

MARK: And you started it all with that stupid first impressions game.

Beat.

LOUISE: Oh my God.

MARK: What?

LOUISE: Mark, is that what that was all about?

MARK: Well, don't say it like it's petty.

LOUISE: It is petty.

MARK: You laughed

LOUISE: Fucking hell.

MARK: You laughed, Louise.

LOUISE: Mark, you are mad.

MARK: What's your first impression of Sarah, Louise – bit cheeky: what's your first impression of Gary, Louise – a good laugh

LOUISE: I like you, Mark, but you are totally insane.

MARK: what's your first impression of Francis, Louise – bit of a bastard, watch out for that one

LOUISE: I'm in bunker with an insane man.

MARK: what's your first impression of Mark, Louise, and you just laughed.

LOUISE: What's wrong with that?

MARK: You laughed!

LOUISE: It was a warm laugh.

MARK: And everyone else laughed with you.

LOUISE: I called Francis a bastard.

MARK: A bastard is good, I would've liked bastard

LOUISE: You're not a bastard

MARK: but with me you just laughed

LOUISE: Because I liked you and it was a warm

MARK: and everyone else laughed as if we all knew what a prick –

LOUISE: I mean is that what that all that was about?

MARK: So tell me now then?

Beat.

Go on.

Tell me now. Tell me now what you thought when you first met me.

Pause. She comes close to him.

LOUISE: Mark, I want you to know that I know exactly what I'm saying when I say this. I'm not telling you because I don't want to and because I don't have to, and I'm not playing Dungeons and Dragons because I don't want to and I don't have to. I really like you. I really think you're a good person and we had some good conversations, really good, but I think you are fucking mental and you're a control freak.

She goes and lies on her bunk. Silence.

MARK: We have to play Dungeons and Dragons. It's important.

Louise?

It's very important.

Are you playing?

LOUISE: No.

Pause.

MARK: Well

I'm going

to have to insist.

LOUISE: (*Beat.*) What?

MARK: I'm,

you know, I'm going to have to insist.

LOUISE: You're going to have to insist?

MARK: Yes. Sorry.

LOUISE: You're going to have to insist that I play Dungeons and Dragons?

MARK: We have to, it's important that we keep occupied, this is actually a really important –

LOUISE: How? How are you going to insist?

MARK: I'm trying –

LOUISE: No, I'm interested. How, Mark?

Beat.

MARK: This is my shelter.

I mean I've not said that before, coz I don't want you to feel…

LOUISE: Are you going to kick me out?

MARK: to feel, no, of course I'm not –

LOUISE: Are you going to hit me?

MARK: No, no of course I wouldn't, never, no –

LOUISE: Are you going to starve me?

33

No answer.

Are you going to starve me?

No answer.

Mark, are you going to starve me?

MARK: It's my food. Isn't it.

I want to do what's best for you. You know. Like when I carried you –

LOUISE: Like when you touched my breast?

No answer.

This dream of yours. In the caravan. What happened after you played the game? What did the girlfriend do then?

We could play I Spy.

MARK: Okay, then.

LOUISE: I spy with my little eye something beginning with 'N'.

MARK: Nuclear fallout shelter.

LOUISE: Yes.

MARK: Look, Louise. I am –

I am going to have to insist.

LOUISE: Go on then.

Fucking go on then.

You're gonna be really fucking sorry.

MARK: What does that mean?

No answer.

Louise? What does that –?

I'm not bothered, I mean –

Louise?

* * *

Morning. LOUISE is brushing her teeth.

MARK: I wasn't.

LOUISE: You were.

MARK: I wasn't!

LOUISE: I don't care.

MARK: But I wasn't –

LOUISE: I don't care, Mark.

MARK: But I wasn't.

LOUISE: Then why was the bed shaking?

Beat.

MARK: I was scratching.

LOUISE: Really?

MARK: Look I was, I was –

LOUISE: Scratching the bishop?

MARK: I was scratching!

LOUISE: Look, I don't care.

MARK: I do, I do care a lot. I would never do anything –

LOUISE: Except deny me food.

MARK: Is

is that why you're saying –

LOUISE: No.

MARK: because

LOUISE: I said no.

MARK: I mean it, Louise, because, that's, this is a serious, and I'm not denying –

LOUISE: You are.

MARK: I'm denying you some food, but I'm not denying you all food.

LOUISE: A couple of mouthfuls of rice for a whole day?

MARK: Well that's up to you, look that's beside, I wasn't, I wasn't

LOUISE: Look, just forget it, Mark, everyone likes the odd wank now and –

MARK: I wasn't! Is this something to do with

LOUISE: Just do it in the toilet.

MARK: Is it, Louise? The food or

LOUISE: Didn't I just say no?

Pause.

MARK: I wasn't.

LOUISE: Well, forget it, then

MARK: Yeah, but

LOUISE: because if you weren't it's not a problem.

MARK: Not 'if' I wasn't, I wasn't –

LOUISE: Well good, then.

MARK: No, because –

LOUISE: Isn't it good?

MARK: Yes, good, but –

LOUISE: Good, then.

MARK: Yeah, but –

LOUISE: Alright, then.

Pause.

MARK: Do you believe me?

LOUISE: Yes, Mark, I believe you, you were scratching.

MARK: You don't believe me.

LOUISE: I don't give a shit, actually

MARK: So you don't believe me.

LOUISE: I'm agreeing, I'm agreeing with what you want me to say.

MARK: Yeah, but you still think –

LOUISE: No, I was mistaken, I was wrong.

MARK: You don't think that. You don't believe me.

Beat.

This is how, this is where, this is where I am

LOUISE: Just leave it, will you?

MARK: Coz you're fucking so…you're so fucking…

So…

You're not quite as…

as you think, you know.

LOUISE: Mark? I'm sorry.

Silence.

MARK: You're not sorry.

You're not sorry, not for me. Not for me. What you think of me. The way you think of me…

He is crying.

Just some fucking…

LOUISE: Mark?

Mark?

MARK: I'm nothing, am I. Just a fucking little fucking...

He cannot speak.

LOUISE: Mark? Oh, Jesus, look I'm sorry.

Mark? I am, I'm really sorry, I was just –

You're not giving me any food, you fucking –

Look, I'm sorry. I was just winding you up, I –

MARK sorts himself out.

Mark, we're friends, we are, Mark, I'm just, it's just here. Being in here I feel...mental. I feel like my mind is being squashed. And I do

trust you.

Okay?

Okay, Mark?

Pause. He is looking at her.

Okay?

MARK: You made me sick in the pub.

LOUISE: (*Beat.*) What?

MARK: You, in the pub, you looked so fucking stupid.

LOUISE: Mark –

MARK: Grinning at him like a

LOUISE: What are you –

MARK: like a fucking cat, all dopey-eyed, you looked stupid

LOUISE: Mark?

MARK: Just fucking standing there gazing at him, gazing, just, you just, in front of everyone, everyone

LOUISE: Mark?

MARK: Francis, fucking Francis, like he's so clever, like, oh you're so fucking clever, Francis, you're so –

Beat.

Sometimes I used to look at Francis. Sometimes I used to look at him smiling there and I'd think to myself 'The only reason you've got any of this is because I don't come up behind you with an ice-pick and shove it into the base of your skull. The only reason you're so wonderful is because I don't follow you home one evening and turn you into a paraplegic by stabbing you in the spine.'

Well he's dead. So who's clever now?

* * *

MARK cooking rice on a Calor gas burner. LOUISE entirely aware of the food, even when she is trying not to be.

MARK: …if you have a society, right, who is good, who is a good, a good

LOUISE: Define good?

MARK: I'm about to define, Louise, if you'd let me, I'm about to define. If you have, well democracy for starters, you know, who feel that people, people can be free and, women for a start, who treat women like people, there's, and where you have rights and whatever, a legal system without corruption or where you can be equal

LOUISE: Where's that then?

MARK: and then you have these other – alright, fair enough, but I'm not saying perfection – you have these other societies that aren't like, that are repressive and dictatorships and where people are tortured

LOUISE: Or starved.

MARK: Alright, starved, they are, and then this first society, the good one, fair enough not perfect because that doesn't make sense, they have all the power, this first society has all the power but because of the way things are, all of our

LOUISE: Decadence?

MARK: Alright, I shouldn't've used that word, but yes, fuck it, decadence.

LOUISE: Decadence.

MARK: Yeah alright, I'm saying that fair enough

LOUISE: The queers and the blacks.

MARK: No, don't because I'm not

LOUISE: Go on.

MARK: No, because I'm not, that's not

LOUISE: Go on.

MARK: Yeah, but no, because –

alright we are a certain way, the people who live in that society

LOUISE: The good society.

MARK: Yeah, the good society, that society can't use its power to

LOUISE: Force.

MARK: Coerce, Louise, the societies, coerce and help

LOUISE: Help?

MARK: them to be

LOUISE: Help?

MARK: better than they have been and give people, the people within it rights.

But now…

Now that things have changed, we can see how stupid
we've been

LOUISE: by not dominating other countries.

MARK: Well yeah, but you don't have to put it like –

If you have power then you should use it. You have a
responsibility to use it. For good.

Beat.

LOUISE: Shall I tell you what I think?

*He begins to dole out the rice onto two plates, a healthy portion
for him, four dessertspoonfuls for her.*

MARK: Go on.

She stares.

Go on.

LOUISE: I think…

I think, it's easy to say things. Alright, I'm admitting that.
It's easy to have an opinion when no-one's testing,

MARK: Exactly.

LOUISE: before, and now that people are dead, I mean I don't
know what I feel, I mean my brother, I keep thinking
about did he get home and is he okay and I know my
friends, some of my friends are, and if I let it that can make
me, I can get really fucking angry

MARK: thank you, which is what I'm saying

LOUISE: but that doesn't, hang on, Mark, hold on, I'm saying
that doesn't affect what's right and wrong and maybe this is
when it matters anyway or something, I mean just because
some nutcase lets off a fucking bomb doesn't mean you
should go around being a bastard and fucking with the
brain of the entire world and saying right you do this or
I'll kill you and your family and everyone you know. You

either believe in something or you don't. Not just when you feel like it. When it's convenient.

He takes out an apple. Cuts a tiny slice off and puts it on the side of her plate. Puts the rest with his stuff.

I think,

He doles out the chilli, the entire contents on his plate, one spoon on her rice.

The only way people can destroy you is if you let them make you become something else.

He has finished doling out the food and now holds the plates.

MARK: That's easy for you to say isn't it. 'Don't become something else.' 'Be yourself.' You've got everything. People like you, have…

People want to be with you. When you walk into the pub people think 'Oh great, Louise is here.' Your laugh, your smile. You know how to dress, you know what to say to people, what to think, what to believe. You've friends, good friends real friends and you enjoy being with them and they love being with you, you don't sit there thinking 'What the fuck and I going to say, these are my only friends I've got and I don't even know what to say to them, I'm making my own friends feel uncomfortable.' You laugh. You smile. And people look at your smile and they think that it's the best thing that they've ever seen. They think that it makes them look like chunks of coal, but they want to be near, even if it hurts them, even if it kills them and turns their souls into pieces of dust.

Puts food back into the box. Chains and padlocks it. Hold the plate out to her.

Anyway. Everything's fucked. Out there. Isn't it.

He hands her the plate. She takes it and they sit down to eat in silence. She wolfs down every morsel, but when it is finished it is only enough food to remind her of how hungry she is. She

*stares at him eating his food, methodically. She stares. Suddenly
she lunges for his food. He manages to get the plate on the floor
and keep her from it. He pushes her away. They stand staring
at each other. She goes for the food again, but again he pushes
her away. Pause.*

LOUISE: Please.

MARK: I'm just trying to do what's best.

* * *

They are playing Dungeons and Dragons. He reads.

MARK: 'You come out of the forest and suddenly the Keep
is in front of you, like a ragged and ancient tooth on the
hillside, jutting up into the night sky. It's covered in vines
and ivy and bits of it are crumbling and the ancient path
wends up to the portcullis. On either side of the portcullis
are two forbidding statues of warriors, suggesting the
ancient civilisation that once inhabited the keep, long since
past. An eerie glow exudes from these statues bathing the
entrance in a dull light and there are glints of moonlight –'

LOUISE: What do you mean 'like a tooth?

MARK: That's what it looks like.

LOUISE: It looks like a tooth?

MARK: Yes.

LOUISE: Like a tooth?

MARK: It's not white, it's just the shape is

LOUISE: Pointed?

MARK: No, not, not a pointed, not a fang, I didn't say fang

LOUISE: It's not just fangs that

MARK: Like a front tooth, a bottom front tooth.

LOUISE: Right. I still don't get it.

43

MARK: Get what?

LOUISE: Why have they shaped it like a tooth?

MARK: They haven't shaped it like a tooth, it's just a way of describing it.

LOUISE: You said –

MARK: That's just describing, it's an old tower, it's just this old tower

LOUISE: Alright, I get it.

MARK: it's an ancient tower that's sticking up

LOUISE: I get it, alright.

MARK: It's the ancient tower of an ancient civilisation long since deserted –

LOUISE: Is it deserted?

MARK: Well, that's what you have to find out.

LOUISE: Can I find out by asking you?

MARK: No, you have to go in –

LOUISE: Alright, I go in.

MARK: You can't just go in.

LOUISE: You just

MARK: Not just like that, Louise, you can't just

LOUISE: Fucking hell, you just

MARK: go in, because you have to be cautious and I haven't finished describing what you see.

Beat.

LOUISE: Alright, finish describing what I see.

Beat.

MARK: '– and there are glints of moonlight on the ramparts.'

LOUISE: Is that it?

MARK: Yes.

LOUISE: I go in.

MARK: You can't just go in.

LOUISE: Why not?

MARK: Because it might be dangerous.

LOUISE: Is it dangerous?

MARK: That's what you have to find out.

LOUISE: Can you just fucking tell me?

MARK: No, because you have to

LOUISE: This is shit.

MARK: It's not shit.

It's not shit, Louise.

You have to figure out whether it's dangerous from what I tell you, from my description, from

LOUISE: Alright.

MARK: from what I've said

LOUISE: Alright, alright!

Can I ask the pixie?

MARK: (*Beat.*) She's an elf. There are no pixies in this game. Pixies are from children's fairy stories and this is not –

LOUISE: Can I ask the elf?

MARK: You can ask the elf.

Pause.

LOUISE: Alright then.

MARK: What?

LOUISE: I ask the fucking elf!

MARK: What, what do you ask her, what do you –

LOUISE: I turn to the elf and say 'Is it dangerous?'

MARK: She says 'I don't now'

LOUISE: Fucking hell.

MARK: but she says 'It wouldn't be too wise to walk into that light.'

LOUISE: What does that mean?

MARK: Look Louise, I can't tell you every –

LOUISE: Give me the description again.

Beat.

MARK: 'You come out of the forest and suddenly the Keep is in front of you, like a ragged and ancient tooth on the hillside, jutting up into the night sky. It's covered in vines and ivy and bits of it are crumbling and the ancient path wends up to the portcullis. On either side of the portcullis are two forbidding statues of warriors, suggesting the ancient civilisation that once inhabited the keep, long since past. An eerie glow exudes from these statues bathing the entrance in a dull light and there are glints of moonlight on the ramparts.'

Beat.

LOUISE: This is what you used to dream about? Being in a caravan with this? A dwarf and a pixie and a tower shaped like a tooth?

Pause.

MARK: She's an elf. She's an elf and you know she's an elf. You're just saying pixie because you want to sabotage the game. If you're not going to play it properly then you shouldn't –

LOUISE: You're starving me into playing it!

MARK: To help you, to look after you!

LOUISE: To look after me?

MARK: You say 'Yeah, I'll play' but you can't just, just accept it and play, you have to call an elf a pixie just to remind me that you're better than me.

LOUISE: Who the fuck –?

You're looking after me?

MARK: Are you going to play it properly?

Beat.

LOUISE: You're looking after me, Mark?

MARK: Louise –

LOUISE: Let's play.

Beat.

MARK: Properly?

LOUISE: Let's play.

MARK: Louise. I want to get on.

Beat.

LOUISE: Alright. Give me the description again.

MARK: 'You come out of the forest and suddenly the Keep is in front of you, like a ragged and ancient tooth on the hillside, jutting up into the night sky. It's covered in vines and ivy and bits of it are crumbling and the ancient path wends up to the portcullis. On either side of the portcullis are two forbidding statues of warriors, suggesting the ancient civilisation that once inhabited the keep, long since past. An eerie glow exudes from these statues bathing the entrance in a dull light and there are glints of moonlight on the ramparts.'

LOUISE: I walk forward, out of the forest

MARK: I don't think that's

LOUISE: Can I do what I want?

MARK: Yes, you can, you can

LOUISE: I walk forward, out of the forest, very slowly,

MARK: Ariel hisses at you to, to come back –

LOUISE: very slowly, taking off my top

MARK: (*Beat.*) What?

LOUISE: I'm taking off my top and walking very slowly into the light.

MARK: That's

LOUISE: I pull my top over my head to reveal my bra.

MARK: They wouldn't've had

LOUISE: My undergarments, I pull my top over my head

MARK: That's just stupid, Louise.

LOUISE: to reveal my undergarments, and still I walk forward

MARK: That's –

LOUISE: And still I walk forward.

MARK: (*Beat.*) The glints, you can see the glints moving on the rampart

LOUISE: I carry on walking and drop my top to the ground,

MARK: the glints are moving, Louise.

LOUISE: and I begin to undo my belt

MARK: Louise –

LOUISE: Oops; my skirt has fallen to the ground.

MARK: You hear a shout in orcish from the ramparts and you suddenly realise that the glints were glints on the metal of the weapons of a troop of orcs.

LOUISE: I walk forward very slowly into the light taking off my undergarments

MARK: Louise –

LOUISE: I pull it over my head, revealing my perfect elvish breasts

MARK: You're a dwarf.

LOUISE: revealing my perfect dwarfish breasts

MARK: (*Rolling a dice.*) An orc arrow whistles past you.

LOUISE: I'm naked now and I'm waving at the orcs

MARK: Right, Ariel runs forward to defend –

LOUISE: I hit her with my sword.

MARK: What?

LOUISE: In the face.

MARK: (*Rolling a dice.*) You've killed her.

LOUISE: I drop my sword and grab my tits

MARK: They start firing

LOUISE: and I wave my perfect elvish tits at them and

He suddenly scrumples up all the papers, throws them to the floor and turns to her. There is a fraction of a moment when violence seems possible. It passes.

MARK: If you want to call me a cunt just call me a cunt.

LOUISE: You're a cunt.

Pause. He sits down away from her. He pulls out an energy bar. Opens it. She watches.

Give me some of that.

He begins to eat. Slowly.

Mark.

Eats, taking his time.

You better give me some.

Nearly finished.

Mark!

Last bit.

You better give me some.

Raises it to his mouth.

I mean it, Mark, don't do that, because if you, if you do that, I mean it, because I'll really –

Puts it in his mouth. Chews. Swallows. She stares.

You fucking –

You fucking –

Pause. She stares, impotent. Walks away, furious. Calms.

Beat.

I remember now. I remember what I thought when I first met you.

Beat.

MARK: What?

LOUISE: Yeah. I just remembered.

MARK: Don't say something just to get at me.

LOUISE: No. This is true.

MARK: Yeah, but don't say something just to –

LOUISE: This is exactly what I thought.

MARK: Louise, don't because –

LOUISE: No, Mark, this is true.

Shall I tell you? Shall I tell you, Mark? Do you want to know?

Beat.

I thought 'Ahhh'.

Pause.

MARK: No, you didn't.

LOUISE: I thought 'Ahhh'.

MARK: I don't care.

You didn't think, you're just saying –

I don't care.

LOUISE: I thought 'Ahhh. Look at him. Ahhh.'

Pause.

MARK: I could really hurt you.

I could really hurt you.

Beat.

I could really hurt you.

Tens of thousands of corpses up there. People vaporised into shadows. No-one knows you're here. I could really hurt you. If I was a bad person.

* * *

LOUISE waking MARK, desperate.

LOUISE: Voices!

MARK: What?

LOUISE: Voices, Mark, I think I heard, outside there's

51

MARK: What, what is, where?

LOUISE: Mark?

MARK: What?

LOUISE: Out there, voices,

MARK: Voices?

LOUISE: Yes, I heard

MARK: (*Getting out of bed.*) No…

LOUISE: I think so

MARK: Are you sure?

LOUISE: Well, I think so, I think, no, I'm not sure but I mean I was

MARK: Were you sleeping?

LOUISE: I don't think so, I don't think –

MARK: Shh.

LOUISE: I heard

MARK: Shhhh, I want to listen.

They listen.

LOUISE: I heard

MARK: Shhhh!

LOUISE: Mark, maybe it's alright, maybe we can

MARK: Louise!

They listen.

MARK: There's nothing.

LOUISE: No.

Beat.

But I think there was, Mark.

MARK: Well...

LOUISE: I'm sure I wasn't

MARK: I mean, down here we can't hear

LOUISE: I know, I know, but maybe

MARK: four foot of earth, I mean

LOUISE: The voice, the sound, maybe the sound travelled down

MARK: What did the voice say?

LOUISE: (*Beat.*) It was a boy.

MARK: A boy?

LOUISE: Yeah. There were boys, they were talking about clubbing and

MARK: Clubbing?

LOUISE: Yes.

Yes, I –

I don't think I was sleeping, I mean...

I mean...

MARK: Clubbing?

LOUISE: Well... and a girl called Chimge [*pronounced Chim-gay*]

I know it sounds, but I'm sure, Mark, I think I was

Jesus, I mean.

MARK: It was a dream.

LOUISE: Was it?

MARK: Boys talking about clubbing and a girl called Chimge?

Beat.

53

LOUISE: Let's bang on the hatch.

MARK: What for?

LOUISE: Get their attention.

MARK: Who, there's no-one out there.

LOUISE: I know, but maybe, because if we could go out

MARK: Stay away from the hatch.

LOUISE: Mark

MARK: That is the most vulnerable part of the whole shelter, everywhere else, four feet of earth. Stay away from the hatch. Go to bed.

He begins to get into bed. She waits, still unsure. Suddenly she rushes to the hatch, begins banging on it.

LOUISE: HEY!

MARK: Louise!

LOUISE: HEY, IN HERE, HEY!

MARK: Stop!

LOUISE: HEY, HEY!

He drags her down.

MARK: What the fuck are you doing?

LOUISE: What if they're out there?

MARK: Who, who? Who the fuck is out there?

LOUISE: I know but

MARK: All that is out there is a blanket of nuclear fucking fallout, and if you open that hatch

LOUISE: I'm not talking about opening

MARK: you let in an avalanche of radioactive dust

LOUISE: I know, I'm sorry, but what if it I wasn't dreaming?

MARK: that will kill us, you mean what if there were boys sitting out there in that nuclear fallout chatting about clubbing and a girl called Chimge?

LOUISE: Well if you say it like that

MARK: Are you okay?

LOUISE: Am I okay?

MARK: Have you had any other, I mean have you heard anything else?

LOUISE: No

MARK: Noises or voices

LOUISE: No.

MARK: because –

Here, have some food.

Unchains box. Begins to get some food out.

LOUISE: What?

MARK: D'you want some, here, here look, I'm gonna give

LOUISE: Yes.

MARK: Here.

He offers her an energy bar. She takes it.

LOUISE: Thank you.

Begins eating before he can take it back. She stops. Stares at him.

MARK: What?

Pause.

What?

LOUISE: Why are you giving me food?

Beat.

MARK: Because…

LOUISE: What?

MARK: You're hungry, you need –

LOUISE: I've been hungry for the last four days, why now?

MARK: Because…

   things, you're hearing, you're…

   hallucinating.

LOUISE: Okay.

   Pause.

   Mark?

MARK: Yes?

LOUISE: Can I ask you something?

MARK: Yes.

LOUISE: And you not get angry?

MARK: Depends what you ask.

LOUISE: Will you promise?

MARK: No, because it depends what you –

LOUISE: What's out there?

MARK: What's out there?

LOUISE: Yes.

MARK: What d'you mean? Rubble and

LOUISE: Really?

MARK: fallout and, yes, really, bodies and you know, you
   know what's

LOUISE: I don't know.

MARK: out there?

LOUISE: I don't know what's out there. I haven't seen it.

Pause.

MARK: What? What are you –?

I mean are you saying –?

Louise?

Is that what you think of me?

Pause.

LOUISE: No.

But is it true?

Beat. He snatches the energy bar out of her hand.

MARK: You fucking cunt.

LOUISE: Sorry

MARK: You fucking cunt, you fucking, fucking

LOUISE: sorry, look I'm sorry, but

MARK: after everything, everything I've

LOUISE: don't get all, because I'm just

MARK: done, everything, saving your, saving your fucking life, Louise!

He grabs her by the neck. Stares at her.

LOUISE: Mark, let go!

He doesn't.

Mark, let go!

He doesn't. She tries prying his hand away, but it's no good.

Let fucking go.

She Struggles more. Gives up.

Alright, I'm sorry, okay? I'm sorry, I'm really fucking sorry, only I had to, I mean I haven't seen, I'm just taking your –

Will you let go, please?

Mark, please?

Please!

He lets her go. Pause. They stare at each other. Suddenly she pushes him and heads for the hatch. He grabs her, throws her to the floor, twists her arm behind her back causing her to scream in pain and frustration. Grabs the chain.

What? What do you what?

Chains her ankle.

Alright, look you've made your point, I'm sorry, I'm really fucking sorry, now please let go.

Mark, please!

MARK: I'm not having you open that hatch!

Chains her to the bunk, gets off. She recoils.

This is what you're making me do. This is what you are making me do to you to help you. To help you Louise, this is what I have to do to you to help you. No more nice!

LOUISE: Mark –

MARK: Why are you doing this to me?

End

She sits chained to her bunk, he sits at the table, wanking, talking to himself, muttering inaudible stuff. He stares deliberately at her, though it is as if she is not there. This goes on for some time. He comes. Cleans himself with the Dungeons and Dragons papers. Sits there panting, cock in hand. He looks up at her as if noticing her for the first time. Looks down. Begins to cry. Starts playing with himself. Gets hard. Starts wanking again, staring at her, still crying. She glares at nothing.

* * *

MARK wakes up to find that LOUISE has a knife to his throat. It is the knife that he cut the apple with, a kitchen or hunting knife about six to eight inches long.

Pause. She motions him out of the bed with the knife. He gets out of the bed. He is wearing only his underpants. They stand there, the knife to his throat. She indicates that he should sit on the floor. He does so. Pause. She is unsure of what to do next.

MARK: We could have a conversation –

Beat.

We could –

God. This has gone a bit, you know, far and, hasn't it? And – I mean we're friendly, and friends and all this…

We could have a conversation, a talk and –

LOUISE: Key.

Finds his trousers, Holds out the key.

Do it.

He undoes the padlock, leaving the key in it, takes off the chain.

Food.

He goes to the chest, opens it. Pulls out a can of chilli, opens it, gives it to her. She eats, staring at him.

Cold.

Pause.

Said I'm cold.

He sets up the stove, turns it on. She eats, watching him. Finishes.

Water.

He passes her the water. She drinks. Lots.

Turn round.

Does so.

Sit on your hands.

Does so.

Look down. Close your eyes.

Does so.

She puts the radio on.

LOUISE: That stays on, alright.

She takes off her top, keeping her bra on. Washes herself, dries herself, puts her top back on. Stands up. Looks at him. Stands close to him.

MARK: There's not much left, we have to be –

LOUISE: Don't look at me!

He looks down.

Cunt.

Stupid cunt.

She washes. Gets up. Considers.

Stand up.

He does so.

Close your eyes.

Does so.

Put your arms out.

Does so.

Up.

Does so.

Stand on one leg.

Does so.

Open your eyes.

Does so.

Sit.

Does so. She goes over to him.

I could really hurt you.

Beat.

I could really hurt you.

I could really hurt you.

MARK: Alright, I think this has –

LOUISE: Get your cock out.

MARK: What?

LOUISE: Get your cock out.

MARK: No.

    Beat.

No. No, Louise.

Pause. He gets his cock out. She passes him some water.

LOUISE: Wash it.

Washes it. She throws him a towel.

Dry it.

He dries it. She goes over to him. Holds his cock. He tries not to look scared. She places the blade of the knife under his cock. Pause.

LOUISE: What's up there?

MARK: What?

LOUISE: Answer!

MARK: Fallout, rubble –

LOUISE: What about the boys?

MARK: What boys?

LOUISE: The boys I heard, what about –

MARK: A dream –

LOUISE: I'm gonna cut your cock off.

MARK: Please don't.

LOUISE: Gonna cut it off and watch.

MARK: Please, please don't –

LOUISE: Tell me!

MARK: I have!

LOUISE: Is that the truth?

MARK: It's the truth, it's true it's –

LOUISE: Is it?

MARK: Yes, yes, please, don't, please, please…

Beat. He is crying.

Please! Please don't!

She moves away. Stares at him. Waits.

LOUISE: Stop crying.

Stop fucking crying.

Looks at the hatch. At him. Thinks.

Put the chain on.

He doesn't move.

Put the chain on.

MARK: No.

LOUISE: Put –

MARK: Alright, Look, Louise; please don't make me put the chain on.

LOUISE: Put it on.

MARK: I won't do anything, please.

LOUISE: Put it on.

MARK: I'll be good, honestly, I won't –

LOUISE: Put it on.

MARK: I don't want to wear –

LOUISE: Put. It. On.

Pause. He puts the chain around his neck. Picks up the padlock.

MARK: Think the key's stuck

LOUISE: Put it on

MARK: I think it's jammed or

LOUISE: It's not jammed

MARK: no, hang on

LOUISE: don't

MARK: I'm just gonna

Breaks key under his foot.

LOUISE: Don't –

MARK: Broke.

Sorry. It… it just

broke.

She stare at him, furious.

LOUISE: I'll stab you…

She goes for him. He dodges the blow, but she comes at him again. Unable to get away he cowers on the floor, covering his head with his hands.

MARK: Sorry, sorry. Sorry, sorry, sorry, sorry…

Please?

Louise, it's Mark, it's Mark!

She stops. Moves back, shaken.

Thank you.

Thank you.

Pause.

Shitter.

*   *   *

LOUISE is sitting over the stove, which has a pot on it. She pokes at the contents of the pot on it with her knife. The stove is unlit. She is wrapped in a blanket, he is not, shivering. MARK watches her. The radio spews static.

MARK: …and there was the time when your car broke down. D'you remember when your car broke down? We were in the Mitre and you were driving because you were off up to see your dad and you were sitting next to me, in the beer garden and we were squashed because there was a lot of us and you were squashed up against me, but it wasn't like that, but it was beautiful, and I was there with Pete and he was being alright, he wasn't being, Pete was being alright, for once, and the sun was going down and I was wondering what you were thinking. I was thinking 'What is she thinking?' And I looked up and there was a star in the red, this bright star, and I thought that the world would be a perfect world if I could talk just to you. And then I thought maybe we were. Maybe on some level our souls were communicating, and I saw these beings of light, you know, the real us, not this corporeal, entwining around each other. And when you went, it was like dying and going down the tunnel and then being ripped back into this world by a defibrillator.

And then you came back. You just suddenly appeared and I heard myself saying 'You can stay at mine' and you said 'Can I?' and I said. 'Yeah. Yeah, of course.' And it was like the world had changed and every thing on the planet was possible. It was a new world.

But you stayed with Mandy.

Silence. She tries some rice. Spits it out.

I told you.

LOUISE: Shut up.

MARK: I told you, it's inedible. It won't work. You need gas to cook rice.

LOUISE: I'm soaking it.

MARK: You can't soak it. It'll be sludge. You're cooking sludge.

LOUISE: Don't speak.

MARK: There's days to go. Two, three days maybe.

LOUISE: Can last two days

MARK: Look at you. Jesus Christ, look at you, at what you've become.

LOUISE: Look at you.

MARK: Look at you. You can't live on rice. Uncooked rice.

LOUISE: Shut your mouth.

MARK: Okay, I'll shut up, I'll just shut up then, shall I.

Beat. She begins to scoop out the rice, try and make it into balls.

D'you remember softball? Softball? D'you remember softball? I remember softball. Everyone there, the whole company and I remember sitting under that tree with you, do you remember the tree, it was like a big, it was a big, and I wish I knew what type of tree it was, that's something I always mean to do is learn the names of trees, maybe some plants, I dunno, but we sat under that tree and this was probably only for, no more than, what? fifteen minutes? twenty at the most? and yes there was drink and yes you'd had a few and yes I'd been doing very well, a home run and I'd caught that, their first batter, I'd caught her out and yes, yes alright, all these things, yes, but we talked, we talked, Louise. D'you remember? We really talked. D'you remember? do you Louise? we talked about the existence of life on other planets. And I was saying how they'd discovered methane on Mars and that this was probably the result of microbes producing the methane, d'you remember? and we talked about what happens if we discover life on the first planet we go to considering there's billions of galaxies, two hundred million stars in ours alone, that it would mean the universe was teeming with life, and it was like we were explorers, d'you remember? it was like we were explorers in ideas, it was like we were the first humans in an alien landscape and I could almost feel the tree growing under our backs and I turned to you and said 'Aren't we lucky.' And you said 'Yes.' 'Yes' you said. And 'I thought I love this woman, this woman, I love –'

The radio suddenly goes silent. Pause. LOUISE goes over to it.

No radio.

LOUISE: Shut up.

She picks it up. Fiddles with it, but it is dead.

MARK: Batteries. No radio.

LOUISE: Shut. Up.

MARK: You can't last three days.

LOUISE: Can

MARK: No food, no radio.

LOUISE: So?

MARK: I can forgive you.

LOUISE: Shut up.

MARK: Look what you're doing to us. You can't last.

LOUISE: Can.

MARK: Can't.

LOUISE: Can.

MARK: Can't.

LOUISE: Can.

MARK: Can't, Louise, can't.

She goes back to the stove, but realising that the rice is useless he has nothing to do. Pause.

Then there was the fire drill. D'you remember that time they did the fire drill? There was the fire drill, d'you remember the fire drill, Louise? They called the fire drill and we all had to gather outside Tesco's and we started joking that this'd be a good time for the weekly shop, d'you remember that? I remember that, and there was the time when a dog came into the building, d'you remember when a dog came into the building? a stray dog and everyone stopped work and

She puts her hands over her ears.

watched, because I mean there was a dog in the building and we were saying, d'you remember, we were saying that Tony was probably going to ask it if it wanted to be a line manager and Tony was a little miffed at that and…

* * *

MARK lies on his bunk fast asleep. LOUISE sits at the table, knife in hand, but her head is nodding. She almost falls asleep but at the last minute she wakes. Panics, looks at MARK, but he is still asleep. She shakes her head, tries to rub the sleep from her eyes. She tries to stay awake but soon her head is nodding again. This time she nearly drops the knife. She gets up, walks around. Goes over to look at MARK, see if he's really asleep. She goes to the hatch. Goes and sits on the cold floor. Changes position, keeping an eye on MARK. Sits kneeling on the floor so that she can't sleep. Dozes out. Shakes her head. Gets up, goes over to MARK again, but he is still fast asleep. Goes back to her kneeling position on the floor. Her head nods.

Lower. Lower.

Lower.

She is asleep.

The hand with the knife is in her lap.

She sleeps. Somehow this position has beome tenable.

She sleeps.

She sleeps.

MARK gets up silently and quickly, in one move, goes straight to her and grabs the knife from her hand. She recoils, instantly awake. He stands there in his underpants holding the knife. She backs away. They stare at each other. He has the knife at arm's length, furious. Long pause. He sags. Tries not to cry. She stares. The arm with the knife lowers, slowly. He is crying now, quietly, head bowed. She stares at him. Pause. He shuffles towards her, head lowered.

She is frozen. He moves into her, puts his arms around her, crying, buries his face in her neck. She stands. They stay like that for a while. Slowly, she raises her arms, returning the hug, but.

LOUISE: There, there

there, there.

They hug, both needing it.

They hug.

He begins to kiss her neck. She tries to pull away but he is clutching her hard.

Mark?

Mark?

His hand is on her breasts, in her hair, while he kisses her face through his tears. She struggles now, pushing hard at him. He lifts the knife to her neck and she freezes. He kisses her face, her mouth, still crying but pushing his groin up into her, against her.

She doesn't move.

Mark?

MARK: My love. My darling.

LOUISE: Mark?

MARK: My beautiful darling, my beautiful Louise.

LOUISE: Mark?

His hands are inside her clothes.

Mark, don't –

He pushes the knife against her neck and she freezes.

MARK: My beautiful darling, my beautiful Louise.

He begins to undo her trousers, yanks them down. He is still crying. He forces her to the ground. He pulls off her trousers and knickers, kissing her stomach

My beautiful Louise, beautiful, beautiful

He performs oral sex on her, the knife now held directly above her stomach, the tip of the blade touching her skin. She stares at him. He comes back up, knife to her throat.

LOUISE: Don't

MARK: I love you.

LOUISE: Don't

MARK: My beautiful

LOUISE: Don't

MARK: Louise

He penetrates her. He moves with increasing desperation, still crying, occasionally saying 'my beautiful Louise'. She waits for him to finish.

* * *

MARK sits wrapped in a blanket and his thoughts. LOUISE is also wrapped in a blanket.

MARK: Does it –

Does it hurt, or…

She takes a sheet of Dungeons and Dragons paper and lays it on the floor.

I'm sorry. I didn't mean to –

It was sort of an accident. I'm not that sort of –

Jesus Christ. Oh my God. (*Winces.*) Fuck. Oh fuck.

She sprinkles rice onto the sheet. It is as if he isn't there. She begins to roll the gas canister over the rice to crush it.

Oh my God. I'm sorry. Why can't you just –

Why can't you just like me? Please. Why won't you like me, Louise?

LOUISE: Coz you're a cunt.

He stares at her. The gas cylinder is not working. She takes two pieces of Dungeons and Dragons paper, lays them on the sheet and places a grain of rice onto one. She lifts the gas cylinder and brings the corner of it down onto the grain of rice. She pours the resultant powder into the other sheet of paper. She repeats the process.

MARK: What are you doing?

LOUISE: Making rice flour.

MARK: Why?

LOUISE: I tried eating it whole and I shat it all out.

MARK: I do think there should be tax on airline fuels.

Beat.

I wanted to say sorry. That's what I wanted to do, when I came out of the pub after you. D'you remember? I wanted to say, I wanted to say sorry. Because when you said that thing about tax on airline fuel and cheap holidays and things I think I sounded a bit arsey. But I didn't mean to. Because I agree. It's the third biggest, you know, pollutant and, I agree, really, so, but I was, we all like a cheap holiday and its one thing to say, isn't it, but doing is, but I wasn't being arsey. It came out wrong.

Beat.

LOUISE: What?

MARK: In the pub.

LOUISE: Pub?

MARK: After the pub. I came out of the pub after and –

Remember?

Pause. She doesn't. She goes back to the rice. She pounds on.

MARK: I'm going to kill myself.

LOUISE: Where?

MARK: Over here.

LOUISE: How?

MARK: I'm going to stab myself in the neck with this knife.

LOUISE: Put a sheet down.

MARK: Okay.

He gets up, goes to his bed, grabs a sheet and brings it over to the table. She continues pounding the rice, a grain at a time. He looks at the table, figuring out where he will fall. He sits down in position to get a better idea of it. Experiments with the knife. Discovers that the best way may be to rest the butt of the knife on the table and push his throat onto the blade. Satisfied he puts the knife down, gets up and lays the blanket on the table. On second thoughts he pushes the edges of the blanket into walls, forming a pool. He sits down, puts the butt of the knife against the table, holds it with both hands and readies his neck. Pause. She pounds on. He stops.

MARK: Which side is the jugular on?

LOUISE: Right.

She pounds. He adjusts the knife so that it will go through the right side of his neck. Readies himself. Stops. Pause.

MARK: You'll die without me.

LOUISE: So.

MARK: Let's go together.

LOUISE: No.

She pounds. Suddenly he comes at her with the knife, but she uses the canister as a weapon and hits him on the elbow. He shouts at the pain but is shocked. They stare at each other, weapons at the ready.

No.

MARK: Yes.

LOUISE: No.

MARK: Yes.

LOUISE: No.

MARK: Did I do something wrong? I mean is there a moment when I could have done something different and you would've felt something different towards me?

LOUISE: No.

MARK: I fucking love you!

LOUISE: So?

MARK: Doesn't that mean anything to you?

LOUISE: No.

MARK: Not nothing?

LOUISE: No.

MARK: I'm going to fucking kill you! I'm going to fucking kill you and then kill myself if you don't love me.

LOUISE: Go on, then.

MARK: I mean it!

LOUISE: Go on. I'll smash your brains out with this.

MARK: I'll win. You know I'll win.

LOUISE: I don't care.

MARK: Look at you. Look at what you're like now.

LOUISE: So?

MARK: I'm going to kill you, Louise. Just say you fucking love me!

LOUISE: No.

He rushes her. She swings the canister, but he dodges the blow. She tries again, but it is too heavy to use as a weapon, and he manages to tear it out of her grasp. He grabs her by the throat, knife pulled back to stab her.

MARK: Say it!

LOUISE: No.

MARK: Please!

LOUISE: No.

MARK: Louise!

Pulls the knife back to stab. Suddenly there is banging on the hatch. They stop. Listen. More banging, deliberate. They stare at each other. Pause.

The wheel starts to turn.

Say it.

Pause. The hatch opens, light floods in.

Say it, Louise.

LOUISE: No.

MARK: Please.

LOUISE: No.

MARK: Please.

LOUISE: No.

MARK: Please.

LOUISE: No.

After the End

Private visiting room in a prison. MARK sits at the table. There is a GUARD by the back wall. LOUISE enters, MARK stands. She is dressed up, but standing by the door, looking awkward, not quite knowing what to do. This goes on for some time. She seems to be waiting for the GUARD to say something, but he is silent.

MARK: You…

You can just sit if you want.

She sits. He sits.

LOUISE: Hello.

MARK: Hello.

Beat.

You look –

Beat.

LOUISE: It smells in here.

MARK: Does it?

LOUISE: Yeah. Cleaning stuff, cheap cleaning stuff. I went to the toilet and washed my hands and it reminded me of this cheap hotel I stayed in in Turkey. I've never smelt that anywhere else. Straight back there. Five years. But it's like if I sniff my hands and try and be back there I can't. You know, it's like I can't

MARK: I know

LOUISE: catch it

MARK: yeah, yeah I know

LOUISE: with a memory or something

MARK: that's funny with smells isn't it.

I don't notice that there's a smell, though.

Long pause.

LOUISE: What's it like in here?

MARK: Ah, you know.

Beat.

LOUISE: No, what?

MARK: Pretty shit.

It's prison.

LOUISE: My solicitor said I shouldn't come.

MARK: Yeah?

LOUISE: She was dead against it.

MARK: My counsellor thought it was a good idea.

LOUISE: She thought it might compromise the case.

MARK: I don't think it would –

LOUISE: Are you getting counselling?

MARK: Yeah, I'm –

LOUISE: You're not a solicitor so you wouldn't know.

MARK: No.

LOUISE: Is it helping?

Is it helping you?

MARK: I think so.

Yes.

Maybe.

It helps me come to terms with

what I –

LOUISE: I fucked Francis.

77

Beat.

I was getting counselling. I stopped it. Didn't need it.
I'm fine. She was very good but I felt sorry for her. She
believed in forming a bond through empathy. Empathy as
a two-way channel. So I would tell her what it felt like to
find out that all your friends and your family and everyone
you know had been incinerated in a nuclear attack and
she'd tell me about missing out on sports day because her
mother didn't believe in competitive sports. Embarrassing.
Stopped going. Spare us both.

MARK: How's Francis?

LOUISE: He's good. He's going out with Sarah.

MARK: Is he?

LOUISE: Yeah.

MARK: Really?

LOUISE: Yeah.

MARK: Sarah?

LOUISE: Yeah.

Beat.

MARK: When did that happen?

LOUISE: That night we were all in the pub. Funny, eh. Then
they sort of messed around for a month or so, you know,
not sure sort of thing, but now…

Beat.

I don't think he wanted to fuck me. I think he was just
being polite. I just thought it might help me, you know,
find out some stuff. I scared the shit out of him actually.
He looked terrified. I never really liked him that much. It
just sort of became this thing, you know. You kept fucking
talking about it.

Beat.

I had a hard time adjusting. First month or so. But I'm fine now.

MARK: Why did you come here?

LOUISE: How big is your cell?

MARK: Ten by eight.

LOUISE: Are there bars on the windows?

MARK: No, glass it's sort of –

LOUISE: D'you share it?

MARK: No, I'm not very, they're worried that the others –

LOUISE: What's the food like?

MARK: It – it's not too bad.

LOUISE: Really?

MARK: Yeah, no, it's not great, but…

LOUISE: It's not too bad, though?

MARK: No, it's alright.

LOUISE: I thought 'I'll go in and ask him to kill himself'.

Beat.

I'm sitting there at home, last night, with this, with this cat in my lap and I thought 'I'll go in there and I'll ask him to kill himself. That's what I'll do.' So I called my solicitor this morning and told her that I was going in after all and I called the prison service and they were very good, I thought it might take weeks, but they sorted out an appointment for today, which is quick, isn't it.

No answer.

I thought 'I'll go in, I'll ask him to kill himself and he'll do it. He'll do what I ask. Because he was going to kill both of us anyway. No matter what his solicitor says, I know. I know.'

What do you do in here?

D'you get bored?

Do you read?

No answer.

Do you get telly?

MARK: Yes.

LOUISE: Yes? That's good.

Pause.

I find telly one of the most difficult things. Or I did when I was finding it difficult to adjust. My reactions to it are completely inappropriate. I'm at my mum's watching the news and this suicide bombing comes on and I start laughing, because seventy-six dead and they're all so serious.

I'm much better now.

Buying food was hard at first because I just kept buying it. I'd take stuff to the counter, hand over the money and almost run out of the shop, like I was stealing or something. This one time I was at Sarah's, there was a bunch of us and I saw this tin opener on the counter and I just put it in my pocket, and when I turned round they were all pretending they hadn't seen it happen and I wanted to fucking punch them.

MARK: Louise –

LOUISE: Don't

say

my fucking

name.

Beat.

I figured out how to make it better though. I just try and work out who I was and I act that. I just act that. It's getting easier. They said there would be a period of adjustment. It's getting much easier. The difficult thing is remembering. I find it hard to remember. And when I do I feel, like,

grief.

MARK: I'm sorry.

LOUISE: Are you?

MARK: Yes.

LOUISE: Well. That's alright then.

Beat.

So you're getting counselling?

MARK: Yeah. Yes. I'm in group.

LOUISE: In group?

MARK: Yeah.

LOUISE: Do you like it in group?

MARK: Yeah. Yeah, I do.

LOUISE: That's good.

MARK: I want to apo –

LOUISE: I think a lot about what makes people do things. What makes us behave in certain ways, you know. Every night I been thinking about this. Trapped in whatever, behaviour, I dunno, cycles of violence or something and is it possible to break, these cycles, is it possible to break... And I'd be sitting there thinking about this and this cat, this gorgeous cat with no tail would come to my door, I'd have the back door open because the garden looks, and she'd be terrified at first, it looks beautiful it really does. So I bought some food for her and the first time she just sniffed at it and ran away, the moment I moved, you know, no sign of her for the rest of the night, and I'm thinking, reactions and responses, patterns, violence breeding violence, and the next night she's in a bit further and I'm looking at her tail thinking 'that's been cut off' and I don't think it was, I think she's a Manx, I think they're born without tails, and the next night she's further in and I'm beginning to get used to this, beginning to look forward to it. And the next night she's in and she's eating and from then on she's in every night; she's on my lap, she's following me around, she's waiting on the window ledge for me when I get home. And we sit there every night and I'm thinking behaviour and patterns and is it actually possible to break these patterns or whatever and she's eating and meowing to be let in. Every night. And one night she scratches me, out of the blue, cats, you know, just a vindictive cat-scratch, look:

Shows him.

see?

MARK: Yeah.

LOUISE: Just here.

MARK: Yeah.

Beat.

LOUISE: She knew she'd done wrong.

Took her three nights to get back into my lap. And I'm stroking her and thinking. Warm, delicate, you know. And I put my hands around her neck. And I squeeze. And I squeeze. Until her neck is about the thickness of a rope. And still I squeeze. And I'm sitting there – and this is last night – with this dead cat in my lap, and I thought I'd come in and see you.

And here I am.

Long pause.

I started the job.

MARK: Did you?

LOUISE: Yeah. A different one though. They gave my one
away. But they made a new one for me.

MARK: That's nice.

LOUISE: Yeah.

Only I'm not quite sure what I'm supposed to do and they
seem too embarrassed to tell me. I thought that it was
just going to be like that for the first week, but it's been a
month now and I don't seem any closer to knowing what
I'm supposed to be doing.

D'you know what? if I'm honest, I don't seem to be that
much closer to knowing what I'm supposed to be doing in
general.

Long pause.

MARK: When were you in Turkey?

LOUISE: Five years ago.

MARK: What was it like?

LOUISE: Why? are you thinking of going?

MARK: No I just –

LOUISE: Holidays, maybe?

MARK: I'm just asking.

LOUISE: Weekend away?

MARK: I'm just asking, Louise.

LOUISE: Why the fuck are you asking?

MARK: Because you won't let me say what I want to say.

LOUISE: It was very nice.

Beat.

It was very nice.

Beautiful actually. I wish I could smell that smell.

Beat.

I was going to bring you something but I didn't know
whether I could.

MARK: Yeah, you can, you just give it to, there's a place out
there you give it to them and fill in a form,

LOUISE: Right.

I thought grapes, but then I remembered that's a hospital.

Then I thought cake.

But then I remembered that's a joke.

MARK: Yeah.

LOUISE: Does anyone visit you?

MARK: No.

My mum. Once.

LOUISE: How is she?

MARK: Not too good.

How's yours.

LOUISE: Yeah.

I feel quite

alone.

MARK: So do I

Silence for a while.

Are you

Are you going to ask me?

LOUISE: What?

MARK: What you came here to ask me?

LOUISE: Pamukale. That was the place, in Turkey, that was the place, just remembered, we stayed, it was…

Haven't said that word in years, funny how…

how you don't lose a word, or…

Beat.

It was beautiful.

Pause.

Mark?

MARK: Yes?

Beat.

LOUISE: Do I look like me?

Beat.

MARK: Yes.

You do.

LOUISE: Do I?

MARK: Yes.

LOUISE: Honestly?

MARK: Yes, honestly.

LOUISE: Because I just need –

I was wondering, you know, I…

whether

I just need to know –

Honestly?

MARK: Yeah.

Pause.

LOUISE: I thought I did.

That's good.

That's good.

Silence.

Suddenly she gets up.

I think I'll go.

He gets up.

Better go.

MARK: Okay.

LOUISE: S'long way back.

MARK: Yeah, yeah.

Beat.

LOUISE: If I come again should I bring cigarettes?

MARK: I don't smoke.

LOUISE: Yeah, but you know; prison.

MARK: Just bring chocolate.

LOUISE: Right.

Over